A Gift
from Vis and Sally Upatisringa
in memory of his father
Hun Kwan Goh

Humboldt Library Foundation

THE GREAT WALL OF CHINA

40°43′N 117°15′E

Part of the Jinshanling
Section of the Ming Great
Wall, at Luanping,
restored in the 1980s

DANIEL SCHWARTZ

THE GREAT WALL OF CHINA

with 149 duotone photographs and 6 maps

Including texts by Jorge Luis Borges,
Franz Kafka and Luo Zhewen

 Thames & Hudson

© 1990 and 2001 Thames & Hudson Ltd, London
Photographs © 1990 and 2001 Daniel Schwartz /Lookat
Preface © 2001 Daniel Schwartz

First published in the United States of America in 1990 by
Thames & Hudson Inc., 500 Fifth Avenue, New York, New York 10110

New edition 2001

Library of Congress Catalog Card Number 2001087393
ISBN 0-500-54243-0

"The Wall and the Books" by Jorge Luis Borges, translated by James E. Irby,
from LABYRINTHS, copyright ©1962, 1964 by New Directions Publishing Corp.
Reprinted by permission of New Directions Publishing Corp.

Extract from THE GREAT WALL OF CHINA AND OTHER SHORT WORKS by Franz Kafka,
translated by Malcolm Pasley (Penguin Books, 1991) copyright © Malcolm Pasley, 1991.

The map on pp. 210–211 is reproduced courtesy of Staatsbilbliothek zu Berlin – Preussischer
Kulturbesitz, Kartenabteilung, Sign.: Kart. N 19271.

Printed and bound in Germany by Steidl Verlag und Druck

40°40'N 117°17'E

Restoration work in progress on the lower Simatai Section
of the Ming Great Wall, Miyun

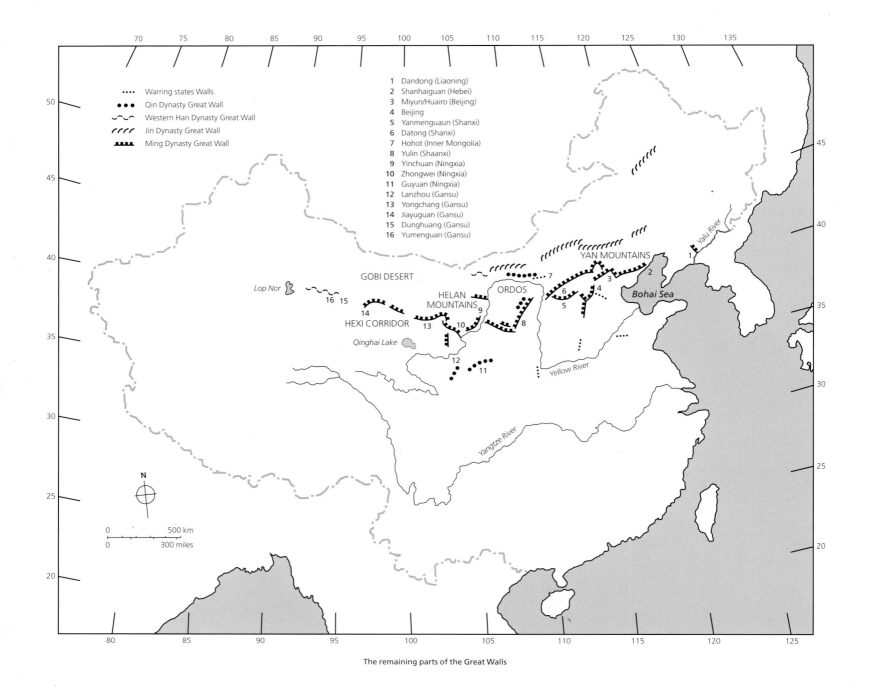

The remaining parts of the Great Walls

CONTENTS

PREFACE DANIEL SCHWARTZ

There is no Great Wall of China. The name stands for a system of walls, erected over 2000 years by almost every dynasty that ruled the Middle Kingdom. The sections known today extend for more than 35,000 miles all told. Each one reflects the political and military circumstances of the time when it was built: the extent of the empire and the geographical location of its capital, the direction from which incursions by the horse-riding nomads from the north were feared, and the expansionist aims of the reigning emperor.

The 'wall' as an architectural element is integrated into China's civilization as it is in no other country in the world. Even after the Middle Ages, China continued to put walls around its cities. Still today, when a new factory, government office block or residential project is built, the perimeter wall goes up first. The tiny, separate eating areas in restaurants are simply tables with walls around them. Often the wall is more important than what it encloses.

So the Great Wall of China is first and foremost an idea. It stands for a world view which distinguishes between 'us' and 'them', and decides who is 'inside' and who is 'outside' and may perhaps be allowed in. It is an idea, a premise, and once the building of the Wall began, at some date in the remote past, putting more of the idea into practice went ahead as though spontaneously, through and across the landscape, despite its harshness.

As a defensive bulwark against dangers from outside, the Wall was never all that effective, but it was a formidable instrument of control over the population inside and over the

movements of the first visitors from the West – missionaries and traders. In recent years, millions of migrants have drifted from the deep interior to the east coast. Now China claims its place in today's mobile international society, on the move across time zones and continents. The complex branching system of walls may stride over all natural obstacles, but it is powerless to block the data on the internet highways.

When I was taking photographs in 1987–88, for the first edition of this book, China had only just started to admit independent travellers. Even then, they could only move between one provincial capital and another along fixed routes, with detours to the 'sights'. In places, Deng Xiaoping's exhortation 'Love the Motherland and rebuild the Great Wall' was being acted on. A cable car was installed and the Wall became a background for commercials and motorcycle stunts. But in between the few stretches with tourist potential and relative ease of access, the Wall, or what was left of it, went its own way, undisturbed, over the eastern mountains, through the loess terrain of the Ordos and along the southern edge of the Gobi Desert.

It was impossible to travel the complete length of the Great Wall from beginning to end. The points marked as such by the fortresses of Shanhaiguan and Jiayuguan are only notional. Whereabouts in the largely vanished eastern section reaching out towards the Korean peninsula I would start my journey, and where exactly in the bright, empty space of the Taklamakhan Desert I would find the last trace of the westward extension built under the Han dynasty, was left to chance or fate, or to the whims of officialdom. Start and finish alike could only be approximations. In between, the maps in history books suggested a generally east–west course. But it was already apparent from flight maps that there was no continuous line to be found at ground level.

In order to reconstruct the idea of the 'Great Wall' photographically, I had to piece walls together. If one dynasty's wall broke off, a substantial piece from another era served as the continuation, assuming that one existed in the region in question. The shortcomings of the photographic medium – standpoint, angle of vision – in illustrating solid fragments led to a technique of quasi-cinematic panning: 'Where does the Wall come from, and where is it going?', 'Looking north, looking south'. Pairing pictures in that way, and having sections from two views overlap, was a device to make visible the Wall's inherent principle: its repetition.

But often the Wall had simply disappeared. Erosion, the encroachment of desert and steppe had overwhelmed it and the construction of the Wall itself created these environmental changes. Reservoirs filled valleys where once famous gates stood. And during the Cultural Revolution the Wall had been quarried to build barracks. In the late 1990s satellite photographs led to the discovery of long, previously unknown sections to the west and in Inner Mongolia, while on the ground sections of the oldest walls, from the period of the Warring Kingdoms, were sacrificed to the construction of motorway bridges.

The closer I got to the Wall, the harder it was to find it, sometimes because of the lie of the land and often because there were no passable roads. When it finally came into sight, it still didn't mean that I could climb it or walk along it because most parts of my chosen route were unauthorized. The Wall's course took no account of the administration in Beijing, which was slowly opening some cities to foreigners while certain regions remained closed. In any case, the Wall does not run near any big cities, but through the hinterland. In China, that is a very long way from most people's everyday life. Apart from my local guide-companions, the people I met on the Great Wall were herdsmen. Once I stumbled upon a corpse.

In March 2000 I had the chance to visit the best preserved section of Qin Shihuangdi's first Great Wall, in Inner Mongolia, discovered only two years earlier following reports from local shepherds. From Wulate Qianqi on the Yellow River, we drove north, into an ever colder, more barren landscape, on roads that, long before we reached the last settlement, were no more than tractor trails between flame-coloured mountain ranges. It was easy to detect the places where travel without a permit would have been halted, had this wall been known about when I first started on this project. If not at the police checkpoint across the road outside the regional capital – it led towards the Mongolian border, after all, strategically sensitive territory, with the line of the border itself disputed – then certainly at the hamlet of Xing Sheng Zhao, where we had to ask the way for one last time.

Nowhere along the parts of the Wall that I had visited thirteen years earlier were the two most characteristic aspects regarding the Wall's psychological impact on the approaching invader so apparent as here on the lunar landscape plateau under the Horse's Mane Mountain in the furthest north of Qin Shihuangdi's shortlived kingdom: namely, the sudden shock of the barrier, here several metres high, built of coarse-cut blocks of black stone, glinting with iron-ore, and the magnetic attraction of the land that surely lay beyond the mountains and frozen river valleys, to the south.

THE WALL AND THE BOOKS   JORGE LUIS BORGES

I read, some days past, that the man who ordered the erection of the almost infinite wall of China was that first Emperor, Shih Huang Ti, who also decreed that all books prior to him be burned. That these two vast operations – the five to six hundred leagues of stone opposing the barbarians, the rigorous abolition of history, that is, of the past – should originate in one person and be in some way his attributes inexplicably satisfied and, at the same time, disturbed me. To investigate the reasons for that emotion is the purpose of this note.

Historically speaking, there is no mystery in the two measures. A contemporary of the wars of Hannibal, Shih Huang Ti, king of Tsin, brought the Six Kingdoms under his rule and abolished the feudal system; he erected the wall, because walls were defences; he burned the books, because his opposition invoked them to praise the emperors of olden times. Burning books and erecting fortifications is a common task of princes; the only thing singular in Shih Huang Ti was the scale on which he operated. Such is suggested by certain Sinologists, but I feel that the facts I have related are something more than an exaggeration or hyperbole of trivial dispositions. Walling in an orchard or a garden is ordinary, but not walling in an empire. Nor is it banal to pretend that the most traditional of races renounce the memory of its past, mythical or real. The Chinese had three thousand years of chronology (and during those years the Yellow Emperor and Chuang Tsu and Confucius and Lao Tzu) when Shih Huang Ti ordered that history begin with him.

Shih Huang Ti had banished his mother for being a libertine; in his stern justice the orthodox saw nothing but an impiety; Shih Huang Ti, perhaps, wanted to obliterate the canonical books because they accused him; Shih Huang Ti, perhaps, tried to abolish

40°40′N 117°17′E

Traditional methods are used to restore part of the Simatai Section of the Ming Great Wall, Miyun

the entire past in order to abolish one single memory: his mother's infamy. (Not in an unlike manner did a king of Judea have all male children killed in order to kill one.) This conjecture is worthy of attention, but tells us nothing about the wall, the second part of the myth. Shih Huang Ti, according to the historians, forbade that death be mentioned and sought the elixir of immortality and secluded himself in a figurative palace containing as many rooms as there are days in the year; these facts suggest that the wall in space and the fire in time were magic barriers designed to halt death. All things long to persist in their being, Baruch Spinoza has written; perhaps the Emperor and his sorcerers believed that immortality is intrinsic and that decay cannot enter a closed orb. Perhaps the Emperor tried to recreate the beginning of time and called himself The First, so as to be really first, and called himself Huang Ti, so as to be in some way Huang Ti, the legendary emperor who invented writing and the compass. The latter, according to the *Book of Rites*, gave things their true name; in a parallel fashion, Shih Huang Ti boasted, in inscriptions which endure, that all things in his reign would have the name which was proper to them. He dreamt of founding an immortal dynasty; he ordered that his heirs be called Second Emperor, Third Emperor, Fourth Emperor, and so on to infinity.... I have spoken of a magical purpose; it would also be fitting to suppose that erecting the wall and burning the books were not simultaneous acts. This (depending on the order we select) would give us the image of a king who began by destroying and then resigned himself to preserving, or that of a disillusioned king who destroyed what he had previously defended. Both conjectures are dramatic, but they lack, as far as I know, any basis in history. Herbert Allen Giles tells that those who hid books were branded with a red-hot iron and sentenced to labour until the day of their death on the construction of the outrageous wall. This information favours or tolerates another interpretation. Perhaps the wall was a metaphor, perhaps Shih Huang Ti sentenced those who worshipped the past to a task as immense, as gross and as useless as the past itself. Perhaps the wall was a challenge and Shih Huang Ti thought: 'Men love the past and neither I nor my executioners can do anything against that love, but someday there will be a man who feels as I do and he will efface my memory and be my mirror and not know it.' Perhaps Shih Huang Ti walled in his empire because he knew that it was perishable and destroyed the books because he understood they were sacred books, in other words, books that teach what the entire universe or the mind of every man teaches. Perhaps the burning of the libraries and the erection of the wall are operations, which in some secret way cancel each other.

The tenacious wall which at the moment, and at all moments, casts its system of shadows over lands I shall never see, is the shadow of a Caesar who ordered the most reverent of nations to burn its past; it is plausible that this idea moves us in itself, aside from the conjectures it allows. (Its virtue may lie in the opposition of constructing and destroying on an enormous scale.) Generalizing from the preceding case, we could infer that *all* forms have their virtue in themselves and not in any conjectural 'content'. This would concord with the thesis of Benedetto Croce; already Pater in 1877 had affirmed that all arts aspire to the state of music, which is pure form. Music, states of happiness, mythology, faces belaboured by time, certain twilights and certain places try to tell us something, or have said something we should have missed, or are about to say something; this imminence of a revelation which does not occur is, perhaps, the aesthetic phenomenon.

Translated by James E. Irby

40°40′N 117°17′E

A taut piece of string aids
the building of a parapet
during the restoration of
the Simatai Section of the
Ming Great Wall, Miyun

THE GREAT WALL OF CHINA   FRANZ KAFKA

The Great Wall of China has been completed at its most northerly point. From the south-east and the south-west it came up in two sections that were united here. This system of piecemeal construction was also followed within each of the two great armies of labour, the eastern army and the western army. It was done by forming gangs of about a score of labourers, whose task it was to erect a section of wall about five hundred yards long, while the adjoining gang built a stretch of similar length to meet it. But after the junction had been effected the work was not then continued, as one might have expected, where the thousand yards ended; instead the labour-gangs were sent off to continue their work on the wall in some quite different region. This meant of course that many great gaps were left, which were only filled in by slow and gradual stages, and some indeed not until after the completion of the wall had actually been announced. It is even said that there are gaps which have never been filled in at all, and according to some people they are far larger than the completed sections, but this assertion may admittedly be no more than one of the many legends that have grown up round the wall, and which no single person can verify, at least not with his own eyes and his own judgement, owing to the great extent of the structure.

Now one might think at first that it would have been more advantageous in every way to build continuously, or at least continuously within each of the two main sections. After all the wall was intended, as is commonly taught and recognized, to be a protection against the peoples of the north. But how can a wall protect if it is not a continuous structure? Indeed, not only does such a wall give no protection, it is itself in constant danger. These blocks of wall, left standing in deserted regions, could easily be destroyed time and again by the nomads, especially since in those days, alarmed by the wall-building, they kept shifting from place to place with incredible rapidity like locusts, and so perhaps had an even better picture of how the wall was progressing than we who were building it. Nevertheless the work could probably not have been carried out in any other way. To understand this one must consider the following: the wall was to be a protection for centuries; accordingly, scrupulous care in the construction, use of the architectural wisdom of all known periods and peoples, and a permanent sense of personal responsibility on the part of the builders were indispensable prerequisites for the work. For the meaner tasks it was indeed possible to employ ignorant day labourers from the populace, men, women, or children, anyone who was prepared to work for good money; but even for the supervision of four labourers an intelligent man with architectural training was necessary, a man who was capable of sensing in the depths of his heart what was at stake. And of course the higher the task, the greater the requirements. And such men were actually available, if not in the multitudes which this work could have absorbed, yet still in considerable numbers.

The work had not been undertaken lightly. Fifty years before the building was begun, throughout the whole area of China that was to be walled round, architecture, and masonry in particular, had been declared the most important branch of knowledge, all others being recognized only in so far as they had some connection with it. I can still well remember the occasion when as small children, hardly steady on our legs, we were standing in our teacher's garden and had to build a sort of wall out of pebbles, how the teacher tucked up his robe, charged at the wall, knocked it all down of course, and reproved us so severely for the feebleness of our construction that we ran off howling to our parents in all directions. A trivial incident, but indicative of the spirit of the time.

40°40'N 117°17'E

Restoration work on the Simatai Section of the Ming Great Wall is carried out by people from the neighbouring villages

It was my good fortune that the building of the wall was just beginning when, at the age of twenty, I had passed the highest examination of the lowest school. I say good fortune, because many who before that time had reached the highest grade of the training available to them could for years put their knowledge to no purpose; they drifted around uselessly with the most grandiose architectural schemes in their heads and went to the bad in shoals. But those who were finally appointed to the great wall as overseers, even of the lowest grade, were really worthy of it. They were men who had reflected deeply on the wall and continued to reflect upon it, men who with the first stone which they sank in the ground felt themselves to some extent a part of it. But such men of course were not only eager to perform work of the greatest thoroughness, they were also fired with impatience to see the building finally erected in its full perfection. The day labourer knows nothing of this impatience, his wage is his only spur, and again the higher overseers, indeed even the overseers of middle rank, see enough of the manifold growth of the structure for it to keep them strong in spirit. But in order to encourage the men of lower rank, whose mental capacity far outstripped their seemingly petty task, other measures had to be taken. One could not, for instance, make them spend months or even years laying stone upon stone in some uninhabited mountain region hundreds of miles from their homes; the hopelessness of such laborious toil, to which no end could be seen even in the longest lifetime, would have reduced them to despair, and above all diminished their fitness for the work. It was for this reason that the system of piecemeal construction was chosen; five hundred yards could be accomplished in about five years, and indeed by that time the overseers were usually quite exhausted, they had lost faith in themselves, in the wall, in the world; but then, while they were still exalted by the festivities held to mark the uniting of the thousand-yard section, they were sent far away; on their journey they saw completed sections of the wall towering up here and there, they came past the quarters of higher commanders who presented them with decorations, they heard the cheers of new armies of labour streaming up from the depths of the provinces, they saw forests being felled to provide scaffolding for the wall, mountains being hammered into blocks of stone, in the holy places they heard the chants of the faithful praying for the wall's completion; all this soothed their impatience; the quiet life of their homeland, where they rested for a time, strengthened them; the esteem in which all builders were held, the humble credulity with which their accounts were listened to, the faith which the simple, peaceful citizens placed in the eventual completion of the wall, all this spanned the chords of the soul; like eternally hopeful children they bade farewell to their homeland, the desire to start work again on the great communal task became irresistible; they set off from home sooner than they need have done, half the village came out to keep them company until they were well on their way; on all the roads they were met with cheering, flags, banners; never before had they seen how vast and rich and fair and lovely their country was; each fellow-countryman was a brother, for whom one was building a protecting wall, and who returned his thanks for that throughout his life with all that he had and all that he was; unity! unity!, shoulder to shoulder, a great circle of our people, our blood no longer confined in the narrow round of the body, but sweetly rolling yet ever returning through the endless leagues of China.

Translated by Malcolm Pasley

PART ONE

40°17′N 124°36′E

Mount Hu on the
Yalu River, on the
Chinese–North Korean
border, marks the eastern
end of the Ming Great
Wall, Kuandian

CHAPTER 1   The other end – from the Yalu River to The First Gate On Earth

Liaoning/Hebei

Stages of Construction
1st: 1381–1382
2nd: 1488–1505
3rd: c.1614

40°14´N 119°48´E

Battle tower guarding
the entrance to the
Jiumenkou passage,
Suizhong

40°14′N 119°48′E

The eastern part of the Jiumenkou Section, Suizhong

40°07′N 119°45′E

The first pass of the
Sandaoguan Section,
Qinhuangdao

40°03′N 119°45′E

Tower and wall near
the second pass of the
Sandaoguan Section,
Qinhuangdao

40°03′N 119°45′E

Dead man lying at the
foot of the tower near
the second pass of the
Sandaoguan Section

40°03′N 119°45′E

First and second pass of
the Sandaoguan Section,
Qinhuangdao, seen from
a distance

40°00′N 119°45′E

The First Pass On Earth,
at Shanhaiguan
(compare with historic
map on pp. 210–11)

天下第一關

39°58′N 119°48′E

Restoring Laolongtou,
Old Dragon's Head,
Shanhaiguan, where
the Great Wall met the
sea. This bastion was
destroyed in 1900 by
foreign powers quelling
the Boxer Uprising

Pages 36, 37

40°12′N 119°33′E

The Yiyuankou Section
of the Wall, Qinhuangdao

40°26′N 117°16′E

Defence system of the
Qianshuihe Section, Xinglong

CHAPTER 2   From the Bo Hai Sea to the Yan Mountains

Hebei

Stages of Construction
1st: 1368–1378
2nd: 1488–1505
3rd: 1568–1582

Pages 38, 39

40°11′N 118°49′E

Damage caused to the
Dongxinzhuang Section in
Qian'an by the earthquake
of 28 July 1976, one of the
worst natural disasters in
Chinese history. Its epicentre
was in Tangshan, 50 miles away

This page and opposite

40°26′N 118°15′E

Parapets and towers have
collapsed in many parts of the
Lijiazhai Section in the Yan
Mountains, Kuancheng

Following pages

40°24′N 117°14′E

A farmhouse built against the
Anyingzhai Section, Xinglong;
a pile of firewood rests on the
ancient structure

40°26′N 117°16′E

Farmhouse and terraced fields
at the foot of the Qianshuihe
Section, Xinglong

CHAPTER 3   Simatai – Jinshanling – Gubeikou

Hebei/Beijing

Stages of Construction
1st: 1368–1378
2nd: 1568–1582

The Simatai Section, Miyun; the Wall on a wall

40°40′N 117°17′E

Battle walls behind
Tower 12 on the Simatai
Section, Miyun

40°42′N 117°09′E

Collapsed outer brick
coating of part of the
Gubeikou Section, Miyun

40°40′N 117°17′E

Tower 14 on the Simatai
Section of the Wall,
Miyun. The ascent to the
summit is almost vertical

40°40′N 117°17′E

Arrow slits in a
parapet on the Simatai
Section, Miyun

40°40′N 117°17′E

The Jinshanling Section
of the Wall from the
heights of the Simatai
Section, Miyun

40°40′N 117°17′E

Curved brick layers of the
parapet on the Simatai
Section, Miyun. In the
distance the twisting Wall
of the Jinshanling Section

This page and opposite

40°40′N 117°17′E

Tower 16 on the Simatai
Section. The Wall
extends in fragments
beyond the summit

Following pages

40°42´N 117°09´E

The Gubeikou Section
of the Wall at Miyun
was damaged during
the Cultural Revolution
and the bricks used to
build army barracks

Looking from the Jinshanling Section towards Gubeikou, Miyun

40°42'N 117°09'E

The Gubeikou Section, Miyun,
with the Lu Zu Temple in the middleground

40°42´N 117°09´E

The Gubeikou Section, Miyun. This passage guarded
the road to the Summer Palace in Chengde

40°43′N 117°15′E

Luanping: in the foreground, the Jinshanling Section of the Wall;
in the far distance, the ridge of the Simatai Section

40°25'N 116°35'E

Curved base of a parapet
with zigzagged layers of
bricks; part of the Mutianyu
East Section, Huairou

CHAPTER 4   As the Dragon Winds

Beijing

Stages of Construction
1st: 1368–1378
2nd: 1455
3rd: 1568–1619
4th: until 1644

40°26´N 116°33´E

Gargoyles protruding from
broken parapets on the
Jiankou Section, Huairou

40°38´N 116°52´E

Beimaguan Section of
the Wall, Miyun

Preceding pages

40°25′N 116°35′E

Looking east to the
Mutianyu Section of
the Wall, Huairou, from
the tower that marks
the sharp turn where
the Jiankou Section
begins to climb

40°25′N 116°35′E

Huairou: looking west
over the Mutianyu
Section, stretching
towards the steep climb
of the Jiankou Section

40°26′N 116°33′E

Looking west *(opposite)*
and east *(left)* over
the cliffs of the Jiankou
Section, Huairou

Looking west from the
Jiankou Section, Huairou

40°26′N 116°33′E

Records show that
the wall-builders used
iron beams, which no
longer exist, to cross
the towering cliffs of
the Jiankou Section

PART TWO

40°17′N 116°03′E

Built in 1345 during the Yuan Dynasty, the Gate of the Cloud Terrace was the southern exit of the Nankou Valley, from where the road led towards Beijing. The archway is engraved with a text from the Dharani Sutra in five languages: Sanskrit, 'p'ags-pa Mongolian, Uighur, Western Xia and Chinese

CHAPTER 5   The Inner Great Wall

Beijing/Hebei/Shanxi

Stages of Construction
1st: 1368–1389
2nd: 1368/1404–1424/1539–1582
3rd: 1436–1455/1491
4th: 1867

40°20'N 116°00'E

Looking west over
the Badaling Section
of the Wall, Changping.
Badaling means
'natural border'

40°20'N 116°00'E

Looking north from the
Qinglongqiao Line
towards the summit of
the Badaling Section

40°20'N 116°00'E

Part of the Badaling
Section, Changping,
restored in the 1950s,
with a stairway exit
in the foreground

Pages 80, 81

40°20′N 116°00′E

The Qinglongqiao Line
seen from the Badaling
Section, Changping

40°20′N 116°00′E

The Badaling–Juyongguan–
Nankou Valley was the
shortest route from the
Mongolian plain to the
Chinese heartland and
the capital city, Beijing

39°25′N 115°10′E

Corner of the north gate
of the Zijingguan Fort,
Yixian, on the banks of
the Jumahe River

39°25′N 115°10′E

Under a broken layer of
bricks, the stone core of the
Wall is visible. The Wall is
part of the Zijingguan Fort,
at Yixian. This defence
system guarded the
western approach to the
capital of Beijing and was
regarded as impregnable

39°25′N 115°08′E

Crenellations of the
Jumahe River Section of
the Inner Great Wall, west
of Zijingguan Fort, Yixian

39°11′N 112°50′E

Wild Geese Pass, part of the
Mount Yanmen Section of the
Wall, Daixian. The steps lead
to the ruined ancestral hall of
Li Mu, a Zhao State general

39°11′N 112°50′E

Record of repair work
done on the Ming fort in
the Mount Yanmen Section
during the Qing Dynasty

39°04'N 112°57'E

The Drum Tower of
The Gate of Peaceful
Borders, Daixian,
is 40 metres high, far
taller than Tiananmen
Gate in Beijing

39°12'N 112°47'E

A beacon tower on
the Mount Gouzhu
Section, Shanyin

Preceding pages

39°12'N 112°47'E

Looking south *(left)* and
north *(right)* from the same
curve on the lower part of
the Mount Gouzhu Section,
Shanyin. The upper half
of the brick surface has
disappeared; the Wall's
inner structure, made of
rammed earth, lies open
to the forces of erosion

39°12'N 112°46'E

Centuries of a river's
spring floods have washed
away parts of the massive
Xingguanwu Section of
the Wall in Shanyin

39°12'N 112°47'E

View of the Guangwu
Fort, built under the Jin
Dynasty (1115/1234), from
the summit of the Mount
Yanmen Section, Shanyin.
In the distance the tombs
of soldiers of the Song
army, killed in 980 fighting
against the Khitans of
the Liao Dynasty

40°18'N 112°53'E

One of the gates of
the fortified village of
Zhumabu, near the Outer
Great Wall, Datong

CHAPTER 6

**Along the Outer Great Wall
to the Yellow River**

Shanxi/Inner Mongolia

Stages of Construction
1st: 1403–1452
2nd: 1539–1548

40°19'N 113°18'E

Crossing the Yu River
at the Hongcibao
Section of the Outer
Great Wall, Datong

40°16′N 113°08′E

Looking east *(left)* and
west *(right)* along the
Second Defence Line at
Xinrongzhen, Datong.
By the 16th century
these ramparts had fallen
into decay and were
controlled by the nomads

40°18′N 112°53′E

The Outer Great Wall at Zhumabu, Datong, is the frontier
between Shanxi and Inner Mongolia Autonomous Region

39°36′N 111°42′E

Shuiguanbao Section, Qingshuihe. From the advanced observer's platform *(far right)* and the battle tower *(far left)*, the movements of the highly mobile mounted nomadic forces could be monitored and signalled

The last stretch of the
Laoninwang Section of
the Wall in Qingshuihe,
before it reaches the
Yellow River

39°38'N 111°27'E

Terraced fields and
watchtowers where the
Laoninwang Section
meets the Yellow River

CHAPTER 7 **Walls in the Cold**

Inner Mongolia

Stages of Construction
1st: c. 300BC
2nd: 221–206BC
3rd: 206BC–AD25/127–119BC
4th: 1190–1196

40°47'N 111°31'E

The Southern Wall of the Kingdom
of Zhao (c. 300BC, Warring States
Period) at Binzhouhai, Hohhot

41°19'N 109°55 E

The Guyang Section
of the Qin Great Wall –
the First Wall – north of
Baotou, built between
217 and 211BC.
During the Qin Dynasty,
boys had to help build
the Wall when they
reached a height of
1.2 metres (4 feet).
Eventually 7-year-olds
were forced to work

Following two pages

41°11'N 109°26'E

Looking north across
the Mazong Mountain
Section of the Qin Great
Wall, Wulate Qianqi

Pages 120–121

41°11´N 109°26´E

Looking south across
the Mazong Mountain
Section of the Qin Great
Wall, Wulate Qianqi.
This was the view of the
mounted Hun nomads
as they came from the
north. They could not
penetrate the First
Emperor's line of defence

40°48´N 111°33´E

Eroded layers of mud
bricks at the Wusitu
Section of the Han
Great Wall, Hohhot

41°15′N 110°00′E

Stones from the fields, thrown by peasants onto the Guyang Section of the Zhao Great Wall, Baotou

Pages 124, 125

Coordinates not known

Left An obo, or cairn, on the Jin Great Wall, Siziwang Banner, under spindrift; *right* snow and tyretracks on the Bulitai Section of the Jin Great Wall, Siziwang Banner

Pages 126, 127

41°58′N 111°21′E

Left The Jin Great Wall under spindrift; *right* the Jin Great Wall, running from the north of China's Inner Mongolia Autonomous Region across Mongolia as far as Eastern Russia. Hongershumu Section, Siziwang Banner

PART THREE

39°26′N 111°12′E

In the distance, towers
in the mist. The Maza
Section of the Great Wall
meets the Yellow River,
Jungar Banner

CHAPTER 8   Across the Ordos

Shaanxi/Ningxia

Stages of Construction
1st: 1473–1474/1478
2nd: 1488–1505
3rd: until mid-16th century

38°20'N 109°43'E

The Terrace Dominating
The North, Yulin.
This was an important
strategic point in the
northwestern section
of the Ming Great Wall

37°41´N 107°32´E

Animal shelters dug into
the Dingbian Section of
the Wall, Yanhuachang

37°37′N 107°35′E

Waiting for a bus at
the Great Wall, Dingbian

38°03'N 107°05'E

The Maowusu Desert
Section of the Wall, Yanchi,
partly covered by dunes

38°18′N 106°29′E

The Northern Ordos Line, Lingwu. During construction of the Great Wall most trees in the Yellow River loop were felled. Erosion and the encroaching desert have since taken their toll

38°16´N 106°32´E

Hengshanpu Fortress,
Lingwu

36°01'N 106°15'E

The First Great Wall,
north of Guyuan, was
also used by the Han
and Ming Dynasties

CHAPTER 9

From the Helan Mountains to the First Great Wall

Ningxia

Stages of Construction
1st: 221–206BC
2nd: 1436–1449
3rd: 1470–1480
4th: 1524–1531

38°08′N 105°46′E

The Qingtonxia Section
of the Wall in Yuquanying
is a barrier of rammed
earth, approximately
10 metres high, running
along the foot of the
Helan Mountains

38°51′N 106°10′E

A fissure caused by
an earthquake in the
Hongguozikou Section
of the Wall at Shizuishan

38°05′N 105°47′E

A less well preserved part of the Qingtonxia Section of the Wall,
at Yuquanying, runs from the Helan Mountains towards the
Yellow River plain. *Above* Seen from the south towards the
north; *opposite* seen from the north towards the south

38°25'N 106°03'E

Royal tombs of the
Western Xia (1038–1227)

37°31′N 105°07′E

The Tengger Desert
Section of the Wall near
Zhongwei is covered
by dunes which reach
almost to the bank of
the Yellow River

Following pages

Coordinates not known

A fortress that once
guarded the now
vanished Wall of
Qin Shihuangdi on
the Liupan Mountain
Section, Guyuan

37°31′N 105°07′E

The Tengger Desert Section of the Wall, Zhongwei

Along the vanished First
Great Wall in the Loess
Plateau, Dingxi

35°49′N 105°59′E

An irrigation ditch runs
along the Muxiajia Section
of the First Great Wall,
Guyuan. Between 217
and 210BC more than one
million labourers worked on
this Wall: convicts, soldiers,
peasants, children. Only
three in every ten returned

PART FOUR

CHAPTER 10

In the Hexi Corridor

Gansu

Stages of Construction
1st: 1372–1382
2nd: 1466–1480

Section of the Lanzhou Loop of the Wall, Tianzhou

38°20'N 101°53'E

The Yongchang Section
of the Wall, Jingchuanzi

38°14'N 101°58'E

15th-century Ming
Dynasty pagoda,
Yongchang

38°24'N 101°45'E

The Yongchang Section at Hedazi, with a Tang Dynasty pagoda in the distance

Preceding pages

38°27´N 101°43´E

The Yongchang Section,
Hedazi

38°36´N 101°21´E

The Shandan Section,
Xiakou

38°38´N 101°17´E

The Shandan Section,
Xiakou

38°40′N 101°15′E

Where the Great
Wall crosses the
Gansu–Xinjiang Highway

38°38′N 101°17′E

A young herdsman grazes
his horses near the
Shandan Section, Xiakou

Following pages

39°48′N 99°08′E

The Yuanyang Section
of the Wall, Jiuquan.
Left View towards the
west from one tower
to the next; *right* view
towards the east

39°48′N 99°08′E

The Yuanyang Section
of the Wall, Jiuquan,
running westward into
the desert

39°48´N 98°12´E

Inside The Strongest
Fortress On Earth. The
western Rouyuan Gate
seen from the eastern
Guanhua Gate, Jiayuguan

CHAPTER 11 **From the end of the Ming Great Wall westward along the Han Great Wall**

Gansu/Xinjiang

Stages of Construction
1st: c. 117–101BC/100–97BC
2nd: 1372–1382
3rd: 1466–1480
4th: 1485–1539/1495–1507
5th: 1539–1573

The Open Wall, on
the southern part of
the Jiayuguan Barrier –
the last stretch of the
Ming Great Wall

39°48′N 98°12′E

The Strongest Fortress
On Earth, Jiayuguan.
For westbound traders
passing through this gate,
Ming China ended here

39°52′N 98°31 E

A watchtower and a
row of fire- and smoke-
producing ovens on the
Yemawanpu Section of
the Wall, Jiayuguan

39°48′N 98°12′E

Corner in the interior
of The Strongest Fortress
On Earth. What earned
Jiayuguan its fame was
not its size but the well-
planned defensive layout,
built entirely of mud bricks

39°41′N 97°58′E

The Ming Great Wall ends south of Jiayuguan, at the 80-metre-high cliff of the Taolai River, beneath Mount Qilian

Coordinates not known

Ruins of a Qing Dynasty
Fortress, Anxi

40°15′N 95°18′E

A Qing Dynasty beacon
tower on the road to
Dunhuang, at Kunxin –
one of many along the
Qing Highway connecting
the Liupan Mountain
in Ningxia with Dunhuang
through the Gansu Corridor

The Yanguan beacon tower. Yanguan was an important fortress and strategic stronghold on the southern route of the Silk Road. By the 9th century this area had disappeared under drifting sand, together with the nearby Tang Dynasty town of Shouchang

Sandstorm approaching
a road construction site,
between Dunhuang
and Nanhu

40°26'N 94°05'E

Big Square Tray Fortress
(the Dafangpan supplies
depot) was also known as
Riverside Storehouse or
He Cang Cheng. Built in
the Han Dynasty, it stands
60 kilometres northwest
of Dunhuang and served
as a granary for Great
Wall garrisons throughout
the Wei and Jin Dynasties.
The walls have triangular
ventilation holes

Coordinates not known

Qing Dynasty beacon tower on the gravel desert track leading towards Yumenguan, Kunxin

40°21´N 93°52´E

Little Square Tray Fortress, better known as The Jade Gate, on the Yumenguan Section of the Han Great Wall, Dunhuang. It guarded the key pass on the Silk Road. Here the Walls from Yangguan and Lop Nur in Xinjiang converged

Close-up of the
Yumenguan Section
of the Han Great Wall,
Dunhuang, built with
layers of bundled reed
alternating with clay
mixed with pebbles

40°21´N 93°46´E

Beacon tower, overlooking
the salt marshes beyond
the Yumenguan Section
of the Han Great Wall,
northwest of Dunhuang.
This was part of a security
system for the Silk Road
and served as a landmark
for travellers. The 2000-
year-old objects found
around such towers
include wooden talismans,
waist tablets worn by
garrison troops, arrow
shafts, lacquerware, a
comb and a child's shoe
knitted from flax

Eroded parts of the
Yumenguan Section
of the Han Great Wall,
Dunhuang. The Heavenly
Fields – flat ditches filled
with sand, on which any
intruder would leave
tracks – ran parallel
to the Wall

200

Coordinates not known

Taklamakan Section,
Yumenguan. An end
of the Han Great Wall

THE GREAT WALL IN HISTORY

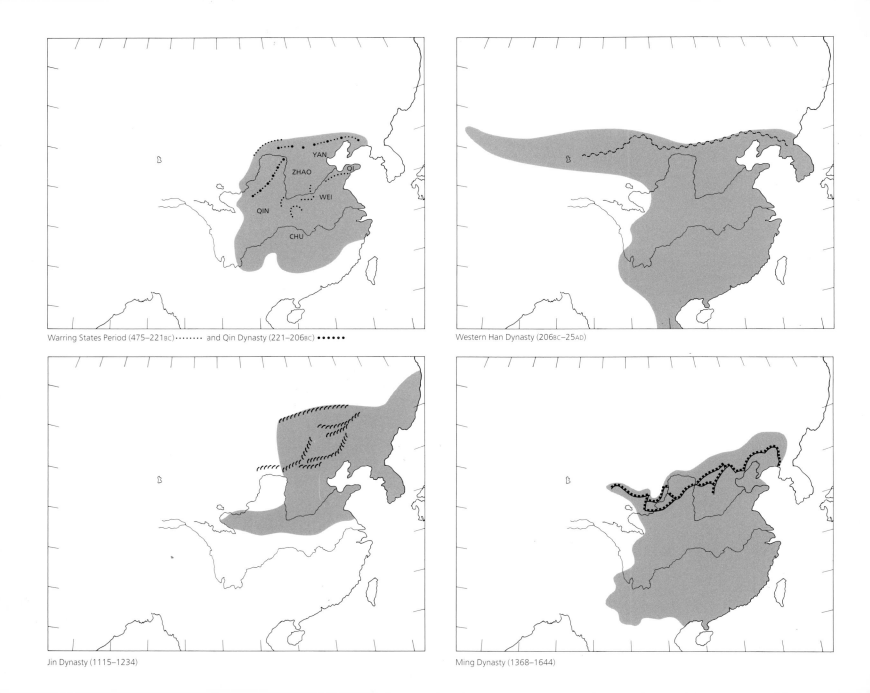

Warring States Period (475–221BC) ········· and Qin Dynasty (221–206BC) ●●●●●●

YAN

ZHAO

QI

WEI

QIN

CHU

Western Han Dynasty (206BC–25AD)

Jin Dynasty (1115–1234)

Ming Dynasty (1368–1644)

THE GREAT WALL IN HISTORY   LUO ZHEWEN

For centuries the Great Wall of China has been one of the wonders of the ancient world. 'There is no good man who has not been to the Great Wall' is a Chinese saying that has come to be used in praise of this great work of architecture not only by all the Chinese people, but also by foreign friends, experts and travellers. In 1987 the Great Wall was included in the List of World Heritage by the World Heritage Committee of UNESCO.

The name of the Great Wall in Chinese is 'The Ten Thousand *li* Wall' (a *li* is a Chinese mile, about one third of an English mile) but it is actually far more than ten thousand *li* long. If we take the length of the Wall as first constructed and add on all the parts built by later dynasties, it is over 100,000 *li*. The scale of construction is without parallel, not only in China but anywhere in the world.

The Great Wall was not simply a defensive wall, nor was it merely a territorial boundary; it was an engineering feat combining defence, communications and other aspects, beacon towers and fortresses. Its many fortified gates, over 1000 castles and more than 10,000 beacons scattered within and without the Wall proper seem to fill the northern half of China. It was extended and restored according to the political and military requirements of each dynasty, whether their capitals were situated north, south, east or west. Today the Great Wall is ever-changing; passing over high mountain peaks, snaking across empty grassland plains or crossing the Gobi desert, rising and falling, twisting and dancing.

A long history

The construction of the Great Wall began in the 8th century BC. It is by no means the oldest building of the ancient world but it has been constantly under construction for more than 2000 years, something that cannot be said of any other building in the world.

The history of the Great Wall is generally divided into two stages. The first stage is prior to the reign of the First Emperor of the Qin (who took power in 217 BC) and this is the Wall of the Spring and Autumn Period (770–476 BC) and the Warring States (476–221 BC), a period of China's history when many local rulers were fighting each other for power. The State of Chu was the first to build a wall in the 7th century BC, then the states of Qi, Zhongshan, Wei, Zheng, Han, Qin, Yan and Zhao all built walls of varying lengths. Some were less than 1000 *li*, some several 1000 *li* long.

The second period of the Wall's history dates from 217 BC, when the Qin emperor unified the country, and in this phase over ten dynasties, including the Qin, Han, Northern and Eastern Wei, Northern Qi, Northern Zhou, Sui, Liao, Jin, Yuan and Ming, carried out building work on the Wall. The greatest periods of construction were during the Qin, Han, Jin and Ming. Work on the Wall under the first Qin emperor extended it to over 10,000 *li* so it only acquired its name of the 'Ten Thousand *li* Wall' from that period. The Han wall extended from the west bank of the Yellow River to the interior of Xingiang province, and an outer wall was further constructed in the northern part; the full extent of both walls being over 20,000 *li* or 10,000 km. Under the Jin, the Wall was extended from Heilongjiang province to the banks of the Yellow River, an extension of some 10,000 *li*.

The Ming was the last dynasty to undertake large-scale work on the Wall (some 7300 km) and techniques were greatly improved. Many important sections were faced with brick to strengthen them. Most of what we see today is the Ming Wall. Throughout its 2000-year history, apart from the dynasties mentioned above, the Tang, Song and Qing also built and repaired the Wall according to their own needs, so we can say that the Great Wall has been constantly repaired and extended throughout its history.

Two points need to be stressed here. One is that in rebuilding the Wall, the aim of the first Qin emperor was to protect his empire from the Xiongnu [a non-Chinese group sometimes identified as Huns]. At the same time, he also ordered the destruction of the walls built by other states, to prevent them from re-arming themselves.

The second point is that since China is a state of many nationalities, many rulers of minority nationality groups eventually achieved the exalted position of Emperor of China. After the Qin (217–210 BC) there were only three dynasties ruled by emperors of Chinese nationality that carried out substantial work on the Wall: the Han, Sui and Ming. Many more of the minority nationality-led dynasties (namely Northern and Eastern Wei, Northern Qi, Northern Zhou, Liao and Jin) worked on the Wall. Thus the Great Wall is the joint achievement of all of China's minority nationalities.

The importance of the Wall in China's history

Beginning with the Shang and Zhou dynasties 3–4000 years ago, the Yellow River plain and North China saw a succession of dynasties: Qin, Han, Sui, Tang, Song, Liao, Jin, Yuan, Ming and Qing. Their capitals and palaces, the heart of their government, were set up in the central Yellow River area, Shaanxi and Shanxi provinces and in Beijing.

All the leaders of the minority nationalities that established dynasties came to the central plain in their struggle to gain the imperial position, whether they originated in the mountains of Shaanxi, the high plateau of Mongolia, the pine-covered Liaoning plain or south China. They came to the central Yellow River plain because the land there was fertile, science, technology and culture were highly developed, and all the conditions necessary to support the spiritual and material needs of government were met.

No matter from which dynasty or which national minority a new leader came, his first main concern after establishing power was to maintain national security and assure the peaceful livelihood of his subjects. The greatest threats came from the horsemen from the north, north-east and north-west. They came like lightning and left like shooting stars and no generals could prevent them. From the Spring and Autumn and Warring States period (770–217 BC) and through the Qin and Han, the lesson that emerged from all these hundreds of years of experience was that the best form of defence against the sudden attacks of these fast-moving horsemen was to build defensive walls. Thus the construction of the Great Wall began and continued for thousands of years. Whether the ruling group were horsemen from the grasslands of Mongolia or mounted troops from the northern plains like the Northern Wei, Liao and Jin, once they had seized power and established their rule, they in their turn all repaired the Wall to protect their domains.

The Great Wall was generally successful in protecting the state and its inhabitants. During the Spring and Autumn period, when Qi attacked Chu, as soon as the troops saw the solid and imposing fortified wall, they retreated without joining battle. In the late Ming, when the latter Jin attacked Ningyuan on the eastern part of the Wall, the Ming general Yuan Chongyan would have been able to hold the town successfully by relying on the Wall had the troops at Shanhaiguan not surrendered to the Qing army: to take Shanhaiguan by simple military force would have been very difficult. Throughout its history, there are many such examples

東昌峪至炸子巷二十里

潘家口至東昌峪二十五里平泉州界

口家潘

房營

閣門

東昌峪

瀶河

小喜峯口

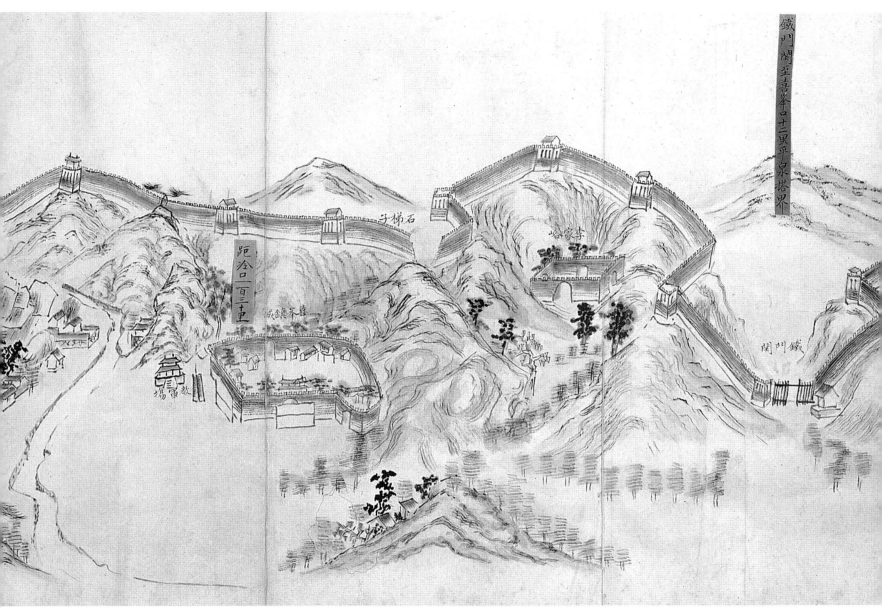

鐵川關至喜峯口二十里平泉塔界

距谷口一百三里

弓梯石

李家峪

喜峯橐鈐城

鐵門關

數軍場

This early-18th century Chinese map shows the Great Wall between Shanhaiguan and Luowenyu, about 140 kilometres (54 miles). Between the various towers the distances are given in detail. The fortress of Shanhaiguan stands in a strategically important position, where the Great Wall reaches the sea. The inscription on the east gate reads: 'The First Gate on Earth'.

of the Great Wall's usefulness in withstanding enemy attacks and protecting the lands and peoples within it.

In its long history of many thousands of years, apart from its straightforward military usefulness, the Great Wall was also a factor in China's foreign relations, in the economic development of the north, in the unification of minority peoples, in cultural exchange and in many other ways. The 2nd century BC saw the establishment of the international trade route known as the 'Silk Road' which relied upon the protection of the Great Wall and its beacon fires to ensure unimpeded movement on the trade route.

The arrival of settlers and the produce of the garrison's fields had a great impact on the sparsely populated and economically backward north of China, and most present-day cities along the Great Wall owe their existence to its protection. Because of the needs of the tens of thousands of garrison troops and Chinese settlers, the culture and products of the central plain and other areas were brought to the borders; at the same time, through the changing of garrisons and the movement of settlers and traders, the culture and products of the north were brought to the central plain and the rest of China, promoting cultural and economic exchange and development. In this and other historical aspects, the contribution of the Great Wall was immensely fruitful.

Military organization and communications

The military organization of the Wall was closely linked to its defensive role. Through the experience of thousands of years, it had become a unifying force that went from the centre outwards to the borders. The basic principle underlying the Wall was 'protect the land by dividing; control bit by bit, in sequence'. Taking the Ming wall as an example, the Wall of over 14,000 *li* was divided into twelve garrisons or military areas, each with a General Staff Headquarters as the highest level of authority, directed from the Board [or Ministry] of War. The size of each garrison depended upon the size of the area it had to control, from 10,000 to over 100,000 men (with a total of over a million soldiers). According to local needs, *lu* or circuits were set up below the General Staff Headquarters, led by subordinate officers. A circuit would control some ten gate towers and a stretch of the Wall. Near the Wall, garrison towns were established as bases for the military personnel guarding the Wall. Within and without the Wall there were also numerous scattered fortifications, staffed by as few as ten or as many as one hundred soldiers, according to local terrain and defence requirements. The most basic form of garrison were those manning the watchtowers on the Wall itself and the beacons scattered on either side, which were staffed by duty groups who took turns to keep watch and make patrols. Within this organization there were seven levels of administration. Military matters were communicated from the lowest level through the six superior levels to the Board of War through the Minister, and thence to the Emperor himself. The Emperor's orders were transmitted downwards through each level; this was part of the system of 'controlling bit by bit'.

Naturally, the coordination of the garrisons of this 10,000 *li* long Wall with its subordinate walls and territory was not without its problems. Military communication needed to be fast and accurate. Thus the beacon signalling system was perfected by military strategists of 2000 years ago, using fire and smoke signals. The beacons have been given various names throughout Chinese history: beacon pavilions, smoke mounds or 'wolf smoke towers'. They were basically similar in construction, a platform ten metres high, made of tamped earth, stone or brick. Around the base there were dwellings, stores for the brushwood and animal pens. If enemies were spotted, smoke signals were used by day, fires by night. The number of enemy troops determined the size of the fires. This method of communication was instant; a message could be transmitted over 1000 *li* in minutes, from beacon to beacon to the General Headquarters, the Board of War and the Emperor himself. There were over 10,000 beacons in all, linking the Wall into a single unit.

Structure of the Wall

A great deal of experience in planning, engineering and use of materials was gathered over the thousands of years during which the Wall was constructed, extended and repaired. There are some singular aspects to its construction and engineering. The most important may be summarized in the phrase, 'Build according to the nature of the land; control narrow passes with strategic fortresses'. This is a saying that has been handed down throughout the more than 2000 years of the Wall's construction. In areas of high mountains and dangerous peaks, the height of the wall is altered according to the lie of the land and the local strategic requirements, making use of precipices or natural cliffs, with gullies and rivers serving as natural protective screens. Strategic gatehouses were situated in the places of greatest threat so that 'one man can hold the gate and ten thousand men cannot get through'.

As the area through which the Wall passes is vast, the geological environment is extremely varied: hence the maxim: 'Build according to the nature of the land and take materials from the land.' In high mountainous areas, stones were dug from the ground as the Wall was built and were used in its construction; in loess areas, tamped earth was used. The parts of the Wall that are brick-built used locally produced bricks. In the Gobi desert, the Wall was built from layers of red palm fronds, reeds and gravel. These methods all economized on transport and human labour. Today, traces of all these building methods still remain; some sections are stone-built, others made of tamped earth, brick and stone or palm frond and gravel.

The labourers who worked on the Wall were equally varied: there were the garrison troops, corvée labourers, military criminals and disgraced officials as well as craftsmen in brick, wood, earthworks and stone masonry. From early on, construction and maintenance were undertaken by local contract and the names of the soldiers who worked on particular sections at particular times can still be seen engraved on stone stelae on the watchtowers.

The Wall today

The historical usefulness of the Great Wall has completely disappeared today; the battlefields and defensive walls of the past can only serve as an occasional historical lesson. But its magnificence and the solidity of its construction remain as an undying legacy for later generations.

Apart from its usefulness as a tourist attraction and an object of historical research, the fabric of the Great Wall, indelibly marked by great natural events of the past – fissures caused by ancient earthquakes, traces of the movements of grasslands, desert and agriculture and the destruction of forests – serves as an accurate and eternal gauge of history and geography. To the scientist it is material for the study of the rules governing earthquakes, the stages of desertification and the growth of forests, and the knowledge gained from it helps to control the environment and maintain the ecological balance.

The Great Wall is a precious national and international archaeological relic and has been the object of considerable veneration. It is now protected in its entirety and important sections have been selected for renovation to be opened to both Chinese and foreign visitors. Apart from the investment of the

Chinese government in the restoration of the Wall, financial help has been forthcoming from all sections of society both at home and abroad. In the 1990s a scientific study of the entire Wall was carried out and in 1999 the 'Great Wall Green Project' was set up. This project is intended to curb the expansion of deserts by planting trees and grasses in areas along the Great Wall. It will also protect the Wall from erosion caused by sandstorms. The project plans to develop ecological agriculture, forestry and tourism in the local provinces.

We have made many films, taken many photographs and published many books about the Wall but we have still not done enough to publicize this marvel. We are confident, however, that the publication of this new edition of Mr Schwartz's artistic photographs of the Wall will further contribute to knowledge about it and make its outstanding visual qualities better known. This volume will increase understanding of China's ancient culture wherever it is published, and will greatly contribute to world friendship.

ACKNOWLEDGMENTS

For V. T.

I extend my thanks to:

The local people, drivers and guides who directed me along existing and vanished Walls in 1987–88.

Professor Luo Zhewen, Director of the Ancient Architectural Expert Group of the State Bureau of Cultural Heritage of China, President of the Chinese Cultural Relics Society and Vice-President of the China Great Wall Society. His passion for the Great Wall also became mine and inspired me again during later brief visits for new photographs.

Zhang Xioyu, Former Secretary General of the China Great Wall Society. Wang Dinkao of the Society for Research on the Great Wall in Beijing. Wang Jincheng in Shenyang; Wang Yuecheng in Qinhuangdao; Peng Siqi in Beijing; Xie Tingqui and Yuan Hairui in Datong; Li Yiyou, Wang Xiaohua and Wang Dafang in Hohhot; Xu Cheng in Yinchuan; Wu Renxian and Yue Bangfu in Lanzhou; and the late Gao Fengshan in Jiayuguan. As representatives of the Cultural Administration, they provided essential help.

The Solothurnisches Kuratorium für Kulturförderung, for granting a fellowship in 1988 to undertake the main photographic journey.

Dieter Bachmann, former Editor-in-Chief of 'du' Magazine, Zurich, who accompanied me on a doomed stretch of the journey. The friends of Lookat Photos in Zurich, who welcomed me among them in 1996 even though my earlier, sparsely populated books might not have satisfied their more journalistic eye.

The photographs in this book were taken between April 1987 and October 1988, with the exception of p. 51, taken in 1990, of pp. 83 and 85, taken in 1993, and of pp. 116–123, taken in 2000.
The prints were made by the author on Ilfobrom Galerie FB photographic paper.